Copyright © 2023

All rights reserved. No part of this cookbook may be reproduced, distributed, or transmitted in any form or by any means, including photocopying, recording, or other electronic or mechanical methods, without the prior written permission of the publisher, except in the case of brief quotations embodied in critical reviews and certain other noncommercial uses permitted by copyright law.

Table of Contents

INTRODUCTION 9

Embracing Vegan Barbecue: A Culinary Voyage 10

Essential Ingredients and Tools: Crafting Culinary Masterpieces 11

Savory Vegan Burgers and Sandwiches: Elevating Flavor Profiles 14

RECIPES 17

Mouthwatering Grilled Vegan Sides 17

Grilled Vegetable Skewers 17

Grilled Corn on the Cob 21

Grilled Stuffed Portobello Mushrooms 23

Grilled Asparagus 27

Grilled Artichokes 29

Grilled Caesar Salad 31

Grilled Avocado Halves 33

Grilled Sweet Potato Wedges 35

Grilled Portobello Burger 37

Grilled Pineapple Slices 39

   Vegan BBQ Beyond Burgers 41

Classic Beyond Burger 41

Smoky BBQ Bacon Beyond Burger 43

Southwest Beyond Burger 45

Hawaiian Beyond Burger 47

BBQ Mushroom Melt Beyond Burger 49

Beyond Guacamole Burger 51

Beyond BBQ Ranch Burger 53

Beyond Mediterranean Burger 55

BBQ Beyond Burger Wrap 57

Spicy Jalapeño Beyond Burger 59

   Hearty Vegan BBQ Main Dishes 63

Grilled Portobello Mushroom Burgers 63

BBQ Lentil and Vegetable Skewers 65

Vegan BBQ Tempeh Ribs 67

Smoky BBQ Tofu Steaks 69

Jackfruit Pulled "Pork" Sandwiches 71

BBQ Seitan Skewers 73

Grilled Veggie and Quinoa Stuffed Peppers 75

BBQ Chickpea and Sweet Potato Foil Packets 77

Grilled Mushroom and Tofu Kebabs 81

BBQ Spaghetti Squash with Grilled Veggies 83

Vibrant Vegan Salads for BBQ Gatherings 87

Grilled Vegetable Quinoa Salad 87

Mango Black Bean Salad 89

Watermelon Arugula Salad 91

Cucumber Avocado Salad 93

Thai Noodle Salad 95

Mediterranean Chickpea Salad 97

Roasted Beet and Orange Salad 99

Southwestern Corn Salad 101

Asian Slaw with Peanut Dressing 103

Spinach Strawberry Salad 105

Irresistible Vegan Desserts from the Grill 107

Grilled Fruit Skewers with Coconut-Lime Drizzle: 107

Grilled Vegan S'mores: 109

Grilled Cinnamon Sugar Pineapple: 111

Grilled Banana Split: 115

Grilled Watermelon with Balsamic Glaze: .. 117

Grilled Peach Parfait: 119

Grilled Coconut Pineapple Rice Pudding: .. 121

Grilled Fig and Vegan Cheese Crostini:......123

Grilled Apple Crisp Packets:......125

Grilled Chocolate-Stuffed Bananas:..........129

INTRODUCTION

The sizzle of a grill, the aroma of smoky goodness wafting through the air, and the anticipation of sinking teeth into succulent bites – the allure of barbecue is undeniable. But what if you could relish this culinary experience without compromising your values? Enter vegan barbecue, a vibrant and compassionate alternative that redefines the traditional BBQ landscape.

Embracing Vegan Barbecue: A Culinary Voyage

Vegan barbecue is more than just a dietary choice; it's a testament to conscious living. Choosing this alternative aligns your palate with ethical, environmental, and health-conscious values. By eliminating animal products from your barbecue repertoire, you contribute to reducing the environmental footprint associated with livestock farming and the depletion of natural resources. Moreover, you take a step towards safeguarding animal welfare and promoting sustainability.

Essential Ingredients and Tools: Crafting Culinary Masterpieces

The heart of any barbecue experience lies in the harmonious blend of flavors, and vegan barbecue is no exception. Here are some essential ingredients and tools to set the stage for your plant-based grilling extravaganza:

Plant-Based Proteins: Replace traditional meat with an array of plant-based proteins such as tempeh, tofu, seitan, and legumes. These protein powerhouses can be marinated, seasoned, and grilled to perfection, offering a satisfying and delectable experience.

Marinades and Rubs: Elevate your flavors with inventive marinades and rubs. Combining herbs, spices, oils, and acids can transform your plant-based proteins into taste sensations. From tangy citrus infusions to smoky chipotle blends, the options are as diverse as they are delightful.

Fresh Produce: Elevate your barbecue game with a variety of fresh vegetables and fruits. Bell peppers, zucchini, corn on the cob, and pineapples are just a few examples of items that can be grilled to enhance their natural sweetness and textures.

Quality Sauces: A barbecue isn't complete without an assortment of sauces. Explore vegan renditions of classic BBQ sauces, as well as innovative options like chimichurri, tahini-based dressings, and sriracha-infused concoctions.

Grilling Tools: Equipping yourself with the right tools ensures a smooth and enjoyable grilling experience. Essential tools include tongs, brushes for marinades, a grill brush for cleaning, and a thermometer to ensure proper cooking temperatures.

Charcoal and Wood Chips: If you prefer the authentic smoky flavor, consider using charcoal or wood chips specifically designed for grilling. These impart a distinct aroma that elevates your vegan barbecue creations.

Savory Vegan Burgers and Sandwiches: Elevating Flavor Profiles

The heart of any barbecue gathering often revolves around burgers and sandwiches. Here's how to craft savory vegan versions that will impress even the staunchest carnivore:

The Ultimate Vegan Burger: Begin with a plant-based patty made from lentils, black beans, or quinoa. Complement it with roasted portobello mushrooms, caramelized onions, avocado slices, and a dollop of vegan aioli. Assemble it all in a whole-grain bun for a wholesome and hearty delight.

Smoky BBQ Tempeh Sandwich: Marinate tempeh slices in a smoky barbecue sauce infused with maple syrup and liquid smoke. Grill until caramelized and assemble the tempeh in a ciabatta roll with crisp lettuce, sliced tomatoes, and red onion rings.

Grilled Veggie Panini: Brush slices of eggplant, zucchini, and red bell peppers with a balsamic glaze. Grill until tender and fragrant. Layer the grilled veggies on whole-grain bread with vegan pesto, baby spinach, and a slice of dairy-free cheese. Toast it to perfection in a panini press.

Spicy Chickpea Burger: Mash chickpeas with spices, breadcrumbs, and finely chopped vegetables to create a flavorful patty. Spice it up with a chipotle-infused vegan mayo and top it with pickled jalapeños, red cabbage slaw, and fresh cilantro.

RECIPES

Mouthwatering Grilled Vegan Sides

Grilled Vegetable Skewers

Serving Size: 4 skewers

Ingredients:

- Assorted vegetables (bell peppers, zucchini, red onion, cherry tomatoes, mushrooms)
- Olive oil
- Balsamic vinegar
- Garlic powder
- Salt and pepper

Preparation:

1. Soak wooden skewers in water for about 30 minutes.
2. Cut vegetables into chunks.
3. Thread the vegetables onto skewers.
4. Mix olive oil, balsamic vinegar, garlic powder, salt, and pepper. Brush onto skewers.
5. Grill for 10-15 minutes, turning occasionally, until vegetables are tender and slightly charred.

Nutritional Information (per serving):

Calories: 120

Carbohydrates: 15g

Protein: 3g

Fat: 6g

Fiber: 5g

Grilled Corn on the Cob

Serving Size: 1 ear of corn

Ingredients:

- Fresh corn on the cob
- Vegan butter
- Paprika
- Lime juice
- Salt

Preparation:

1. Peel back the corn husks without removing them.
2. Remove the silk from the corn.
3. Mix vegan butter, paprika, lime juice, and salt.
4. Brush the mixture onto the corn.
5. Pull the husks back up and grill for about 15-20 minutes, turning occasionally.

Nutritional Information (per serving):

Calories: 150

Carbohydrates: 25g

Protein: 3g

Fat: 7g

Fiber: 4g

Grilled Stuffed Portobello Mushrooms

Serving Size: 2 mushrooms

Ingredients:

- Large portobello mushrooms
- Spinach
- Sun-dried tomatoes
- Vegan cheese
- Balsamic vinegar
- Olive oil
- Garlic powder
- Salt and pepper

Preparation:

1. Remove the stems from the mushrooms.
2. Mix spinach, sun-dried tomatoes, vegan cheese, balsamic vinegar, olive oil, garlic powder, salt, and pepper.
3. Stuff the mushroom caps with the mixture.
4. Grill for 10-12 minutes until the mushrooms are tender and the cheese is melted.

Nutritional Information (per serving):

Calories: 180

Carbohydrates: 10g

Protein: 8g

Fat: 13g

Fiber: 3g

Grilled Asparagus

Serving Size: 1/2 pound

Ingredients:

- Asparagus spears
- Olive oil
- Lemon zest
- Garlic powder
- Salt and pepper

Preparation:

1. Trim the tough ends of the asparagus.
2. Toss asparagus with olive oil, lemon zest, garlic powder, salt, and pepper.
3. Grill for 5-7 minutes until tender and slightly charred.

Nutritional Information (per serving):

Calories: 80

Carbohydrates: 7g

Protein: 4g

Fat: 6g

Fiber: 3g

Grilled Artichokes

Serving Size: 1 artichoke

Ingredients:

- Fresh artichokes
- Lemon juice
- Olive oil
- Minced garlic
- Salt and pepper

Preparation:

1. Cut off the top of the artichoke and trim the sharp tips of the leaves.
2. Steam the artichokes until slightly tender.
3. Mix lemon juice, olive oil, minced garlic, salt, and pepper.
4. Brush the mixture onto the artichokes.
5. Grill for 10-15 minutes until the leaves are crispy and slightly charred.

Nutritional Information (per serving):

Calories: 90

Carbohydrates: 20g

Protein: 4g

Fat: 1g

Fiber: 10g

Grilled Caesar Salad

Serving Size: 1 salad

Ingredients:

- Romaine lettuce hearts
- Vegan Caesar dressing
- Croutons
- Vegan parmesan cheese

Preparation:

1. Cut romaine hearts in half lengthwise, leaving the core intact.
2. Brush with vegan Caesar dressing.
3. Grill for 2-3 minutes on each side until lightly charred.
4. Top with croutons and vegan parmesan cheese.

Nutritional Information (per serving):

Calories: 180

Carbohydrates: 15g

Protein: 4g

Fat: 12g

Fiber: 6g

Grilled Avocado Halves

Serving Size: 1 avocado half

Ingredients:

- Ripe avocados
- Lime juice
- Olive oil
- Red pepper flakes
- Salt and pepper

Preparation:

1. Cut avocados in half and remove the pit.
2. Brush with lime juice and olive oil.
3. Sprinkle with red pepper flakes, salt, and pepper.
4. Grill for 2-3 minutes on each side until grill marks appear.

Nutritional Information (per serving):

Calories: 120

Carbohydrates: 6g

Protein: 2g

Fat: 11g

Fiber: 5g

Grilled Sweet Potato Wedges

Serving Size: 1/2 sweet potato

Ingredients:

- Sweet potatoes
- Olive oil
- Smoked paprika
- Cumin
- Salt and pepper

Preparation:

1. Cut sweet potatoes into wedges.
2. Toss with olive oil, smoked paprika, cumin, salt, and pepper.
3. Grill for 8-10 minutes on each side until tender and slightly crispy.

Nutritional Information (per serving):

Calories: 120

Carbohydrates: 25g

Protein: 2g

Fat: 2g

Fiber: 4g

Grilled Portobello Burger

Serving Size: 1 burger

Ingredients:

- Large portobello mushroom caps
- Buns
- Vegan mayo
- Lettuce
- Tomato slices
- Red onion slices
- Pickles

Preparation:

1. Remove the stems from the mushroom caps.
2. Brush with olive oil, salt, and pepper.
3. Grill for 4-5 minutes on each side until tender.
4. Toast buns on the grill.
5. Assemble the burgers with mushroom caps, vegan mayo, lettuce, tomato slices, red onion slices, and pickles.

Nutritional Information (per serving):

Calories: 250

Carbohydrates: 40g

Protein: 7g

Fat: 6g

Fiber: 5g

Grilled Pineapple Slices

Serving Size: 2 pineapple slices

Ingredients:

- Fresh pineapple slices
- Brown sugar
- Cinnamon

Preparation:

1. Sprinkle pineapple slices with brown sugar and cinnamon.
2. Grill for 2-3 minutes on each side until caramelized and grill marks appear.

Nutritional Information (per serving):

Calories: 100

Carbohydrates: 25g

Protein: 1g

Fat: 0g

Fiber: 2g

Vegan BBQ Beyond Burgers

Classic Beyond Burger

Serving: 1 burger

Ingredients:

- 1 Beyond Burger patty
- 1 vegan hamburger bun
- Lettuce, tomato, onion, and pickles for garnish
- Vegan cheese (optional)
- BBQ sauce

Preparation:

1. Preheat the grill.
2. Cook the Beyond Burger patty according to package instructions.
3. Toast the bun on the grill.
4. Assemble the burger with lettuce, tomato, onion, pickles, and vegan cheese.
5. Drizzle with BBQ sauce and serve.

Smoky BBQ Bacon Beyond Burger

Serving: 1 burger

Ingredients:

- 1 Beyond Burger patty
- 1 vegan hamburger bun
- Vegan bacon strips
- 1 tablespoon BBQ seasoning
- Red onion rings
- Lettuce

Preparation:

1. Preheat the grill.
2. Season the Beyond Burger patty with BBQ seasoning.
3. Cook the patty on the grill and cook the vegan bacon strips until crispy.
4. Toast the bun on the grill.
5. Assemble the burger with lettuce, Beyond Burger patty, vegan bacon, onion rings.
6. Serve with your favorite vegan BBQ sauce.

Southwest Beyond Burger

Serving: 1 burger

Ingredients:

- 1 Beyond Burger patty
- 1 vegan hamburger bun
- 1/4 cup corn kernels
- 1/4 cup black beans, mashed
- Sliced avocado
- Salsa

Preparation:

1. Preheat the grill.
2. Cook the Beyond Burger patty according to package instructions.
3. Toast the bun on the grill.
4. Mix corn and mashed black beans together.
5. Assemble the burger with the Beyond Burger patty, corn and black bean mixture, sliced avocado, and salsa.
6. Serve with a side of grilled corn on the cob.

Hawaiian Beyond Burger

Serving: 1 burger

Ingredients:

- 1 Beyond Burger patty
- 1 vegan hamburger bun
- Pineapple slice
- Teriyaki sauce
- Lettuce
- Red onion slices

Preparation:

1. Preheat the grill.
2. Cook the Beyond Burger patty according to package instructions.
3. Grill the pineapple slice until it has grill marks.
4. Toast the bun on the grill.
5. Assemble the burger with Beyond Burger patty, grilled pineapple, teriyaki sauce, lettuce, and red onion slices.
6. Serve with a side of sweet potato fries.

BBQ Mushroom Melt Beyond Burger

Serving: 1 burger

Ingredients:

- 1 Beyond Burger patty
- 1 vegan hamburger bun
- BBQ sauce
- Sautéed mushrooms
- Vegan mozzarella cheese
- Caramelized onions

Preparation:

1. Preheat the grill.
2. Cook the Beyond Burger patty according to package instructions.
3. Sauté mushrooms and caramelize onions.
4. Toast the bun on the grill.
5. Assemble the burger with Beyond Burger patty, sautéed mushrooms, caramelized onions, and vegan mozzarella.
6. Drizzle with BBQ sauce and serve.

Beyond Guacamole Burger

Serving: 1 burger

Ingredients:

- 1 Beyond Burger patty
- 1 vegan hamburger bun
- Guacamole
- Sliced tomatoes
- Red onion rings
- Lettuce

Preparation:

1. Preheat the grill.
2. Cook the Beyond Burger patty according to package instructions.
3. Toast the bun on the grill.
4. Assemble the burger with Beyond Burger patty, guacamole, sliced tomatoes, red onion rings, and lettuce.
5. Serve with a side of vegan coleslaw.

Beyond BBQ Ranch Burger

Serving: 1 burger

Ingredients:

- 1 Beyond Burger patty
- 1 vegan hamburger bun
- Vegan ranch dressing
- BBQ sauce
- Vegan cheddar cheese slice
- Crispy fried onions

Preparation:

1. Preheat the grill.
2. Cook the Beyond Burger patty according to package instructions.
3. Toast the bun on the grill.
4. Assemble the burger with Beyond Burger patty, vegan cheddar cheese, crispy fried onions, vegan ranch dressing, and BBQ sauce.
5. Serve with a side of baked sweet potato fries.

Beyond Mediterranean Burger

Serving: 1 burger

Ingredients:

- 1 Beyond Burger patty
- 1 vegan hamburger bun
- Hummus
- Sliced cucumber
- Sliced red bell pepper
- Kalamata olives
- Red onion slices
- Baby spinach

Preparation:

1. Preheat the grill.
2. Cook the Beyond Burger patty according to package instructions.
3. Toast the bun on the grill.
4. Assemble the burger with Beyond Burger patty, hummus, cucumber slices, red bell pepper slices, kalamata olives, red onion slices, and baby spinach.
5. Serve with a side of quinoa salad.

BBQ Beyond Burger Wrap

Serving: 1 wrap

Ingredients:

- 1 Beyond Burger patty
- Large vegan tortilla wrap
- Coleslaw
- BBQ sauce
- Sliced red onion
- Sliced dill pickles

Preparation:

1. Preheat the grill.
2. Cook the Beyond Burger patty according to package instructions.
3. Warm the tortilla wrap.
4. Assemble the wrap with Beyond Burger patty, coleslaw, BBQ sauce, sliced red onion, and dill pickles.
5. Wrap tightly and serve.

Spicy Jalapeño Beyond Burger

Serving: 1 burger

Ingredients:

- 1 Beyond Burger patty
- 1 vegan hamburger bun
- Spicy vegan mayo
- Sliced jalapeños
- Vegan pepper jack cheese slice
- Lettuce

Preparation:

1. Preheat the grill.
2. Cook the Beyond Burger patty according to package instructions.
3. Toast the bun on the grill.
4. Assemble the burger with Beyond Burger patty, spicy vegan mayo, sliced

jalapeños, vegan pepper jack cheese, and lettuce.

5. Serve with a side of baked potato wedges.

Nutritional Information:

Please note that nutritional values can vary based on specific brands and portion sizes. The values below are approximate and based on common vegan ingredients.

Nutritional values per serving (including bun and toppings):

Calories: Varies (typically around 400-500 calories)

Protein: Approximately 20-25g

Carbohydrates: Approximately 30-40g

Dietary Fiber: Approximately 5-8g

Fat: Approximately 20-25g

Saturated Fat: Varies (typically 3-5g)

Sodium: Varies (typically 600-800mg)

Hearty Vegan BBQ Main Dishes

Grilled Portobello Mushroom Burgers

Serving: 4 burgers

Ingredients:

- 4 large portobello mushrooms, stems removed
- 1/4 cup balsamic vinegar
- 2 tbsp olive oil
- 2 cloves garlic, minced
- Salt and pepper to taste

Preparation:

1. Whisk together balsamic vinegar, olive oil, garlic, salt, and pepper.
2. Marinate mushrooms in the mixture for 30 minutes.
3. Grill mushrooms over medium-high heat for 5-6 minutes per side.
4. Serve in burger buns with your favorite toppings.

Nutritional Information (per serving):

Calories: 120

Protein: 4g

Carbohydrates: 10g

Fat: 8g

Fiber: 2g

BBQ Lentil and Vegetable Skewers

Serving: 4 skewers

Ingredients:

- 1 cup cooked green lentils
- Assorted vegetables (bell peppers, zucchini, red onion, cherry tomatoes)
- 1/4 cup BBQ sauce
- 2 tbsp olive oil
- Salt and pepper to taste

Preparation:

1. Preheat the grill.
2. Thread lentils and vegetables onto skewers.
3. Mix BBQ sauce, olive oil, salt, and pepper.
4. Brush skewers with sauce mixture and grill for 8-10 minutes, turning occasionally.

Nutritional Information (per serving):

Calories: 220

Protein: 10g

Carbohydrates: 35g

Fat: 5g

Fiber: 12g

Vegan BBQ Tempeh Ribs

Serving: 2 servings

Ingredients:

- 1 block tempeh, cut into rib-sized pieces
- 1/2 cup BBQ sauce
- 2 tbsp soy sauce
- 1 tbsp maple syrup
- 1 tsp liquid smoke

Preparation:

1. Whisk together BBQ sauce, soy sauce, maple syrup, and liquid smoke.
2. Marinate tempeh in the mixture for at least 1 hour.
3. Grill tempeh ribs over medium heat, basting with extra marinade, for 3-4 minutes per side.
4. Serve with additional BBQ sauce.

Nutritional Information (per serving):

Calories: 320

Protein: 20g

Carbohydrates: 35g

Fat: 12g

Fiber: 5g

Smoky BBQ Tofu Steaks

Serving: 4 servings

Ingredients:

- 1 block extra-firm tofu, sliced into steaks
- 1/2 cup BBQ sauce
- 2 tbsp olive oil
- 2 tsp smoked paprika
- Salt and pepper to taste

Preparation:

1. Combine BBQ sauce, olive oil, smoked paprika, salt, and pepper.
2. Marinate tofu steaks for 1-2 hours.
3. Grill tofu over medium-high heat for 4-5 minutes per side.
4. Brush with additional marinade while grilling.
5. Serve with grilled veggies.

Nutritional Information (per serving):

Calories: 240

Protein: 14g

Carbohydrates: 20g

Fat: 12g

Fiber: 3g

Jackfruit Pulled "Pork" Sandwiches

Serving: 4 sandwiches

Ingredients:

- 2 cans young jackfruit in water or brine, drained and rinsed
- 1 cup BBQ sauce
- 1 tbsp olive oil
- 1 onion, sliced
- 2 cloves garlic, minced
- Salt and pepper to taste

Preparation:

1. Heat olive oil in a pan and sauté onion and garlic until soft.
2. Add jackfruit and cook for 5 minutes, breaking it apart with a fork.
3. Add BBQ sauce, salt, and pepper. Simmer for 15-20 minutes.
4. Serve on whole wheat buns with coleslaw.

Nutritional Information (per serving):

Calories: 350

Protein: 6g

Carbohydrates: 70g

Fat: 6g

Fiber: 8g

BBQ Seitan Skewers

Serving: 3 skewers

Ingredients:

- 1 cup seitan pieces
- Assorted vegetables (bell peppers, red onion, cherry tomatoes)
- 1/4 cup BBQ sauce
- 2 tbsp olive oil
- 1 tsp garlic powder
- Salt and pepper to taste

Preparation:

1. Preheat the grill.
2. Thread seitan and vegetables onto skewers.
3. Mix BBQ sauce, olive oil, garlic powder, salt, and pepper.
4. Brush skewers with sauce mixture and grill for 6-8 minutes, turning occasionally.

Nutritional Information (per serving):

Calories: 280

Protein: 20g

Carbohydrates: 20g

Fat: 12g

Fiber: 5g

Grilled Veggie and Quinoa Stuffed Peppers

Serving: 4 stuffed peppers

Ingredients:

- 4 bell peppers, halved and seeded
- 1 cup cooked quinoa
- Assorted grilled vegetables (zucchini, eggplant, red onion)
- 1/2 cup tomato sauce
- 1 tsp dried oregano
- Salt and pepper to taste

Preparation:

1. Preheat the grill.
2. Grill bell pepper halves until slightly charred.
3. Mix quinoa, grilled vegetables, tomato sauce, oregano, salt, and pepper.
4. Stuff the pepper halves with the quinoa mixture.
5. Grill stuffed peppers for 10 minutes until heated through.

Nutritional Information (per serving):

Calories: 220

Protein: 7g

Carbohydrates: 40g

Fat: 3g

Fiber: 8g

BBQ Chickpea and Sweet Potato Foil Packets

Serving: 2 packets

Ingredients:

- 1 can chickpeas, drained and rinsed
- 1 large sweet potato, diced
- 1/4 cup BBQ sauce
- 1 tbsp olive oil
- 1 tsp smoked paprika
- Salt and pepper to taste

Preparation:

1. Preheat the grill.
2. Mix chickpeas, sweet potato, BBQ sauce, olive oil, smoked paprika, salt, and pepper.
3. Divide mixture between two large sheets of aluminum foil.
4. Fold the foil to create sealed packets.
5. Grill packets over medium heat for 20-25 minutes, until sweet potatoes are tender.

Nutritional Information (per serving):

Calories: 380

Protein: 12g

Carbohydrates: 65g

Fat: 8g

Fiber: 12g

Grilled Mushroom and Tofu Kebabs

Serving: 3 kebabs

Ingredients:

- 1 cup button mushrooms
- 1 block extra-firm tofu, cubed
- Assorted vegetables (bell peppers, red onion, zucchini)
- 1/4 cup balsamic vinegar
- 2 tbsp soy sauce
- 1 tbsp maple syrup
- 2 cloves garlic, minced

Preparation:

1. Preheat the grill.
2. Thread mushrooms, tofu, and vegetables onto skewers.
3. Mix balsamic vinegar, soy sauce, maple syrup, and garlic.
4. Brush skewers with marinade and grill for 8-10 minutes, turning occasionally.

Nutritional Information (per serving):

Calories: 230

Protein: 18g

Carbohydrates: 20g

Fat: 8g

Fiber: 4g

BBQ Spaghetti Squash with Grilled Veggies

Serving: 2 servings

Ingredients:

- 1 medium spaghetti squash
- Assorted grilled vegetables (bell peppers, zucchini, red onion)
- 1/2 cup BBQ sauce
- 2 tbsp olive oil
- 1 tsp dried thyme
- Salt and pepper to taste

Preparation:

1. Preheat the grill.
2. Cut spaghetti squash in half lengthwise and scoop out the seeds.
3. Brush the flesh with olive oil, thyme, salt, and pepper.
4. Grill the squash halves for 25-30 minutes until tender.
5. Use a fork to scrape out the spaghetti-like strands.
6. Mix grilled vegetables and BBQ sauce. Serve over spaghetti squash.

Nutritional Information (per serving):

Calories: 280

Protein: 4g

Carbohydrates: 50g

Fat: 8g

Fiber: 10g

Vibrant Vegan Salads for BBQ Gatherings

Grilled Vegetable Quinoa Salad

Serving: 6

Ingredients:

- 1 cup quinoa, cooked and cooled
- Assorted grilled vegetables (zucchini, bell peppers, red onion, etc.)
- 1/4 cup fresh parsley, chopped
- 1/4 cup lemon juice
- 2 tbsp olive oil
- Salt and pepper to taste

Preparation:

1. Toss cooked quinoa and grilled vegetables together in a large bowl.
2. In a small bowl, whisk together lemon juice, olive oil, salt, and pepper.
3. Drizzle the dressing over the quinoa and vegetables. Add chopped parsley and toss gently.

Nutritional Information (per serving):

Calories: ~220

Protein: 6g

Carbohydrates: 35g

Fat: 7g

Mango Black Bean Salad

Serving: 8

Ingredients:

- 2 cups cooked black beans, drained and rinsed
- 2 ripe mangoes, diced
- 1 red bell pepper, diced
- 1/2 red onion, finely chopped
- 1/4 cup fresh cilantro, chopped
- Juice of 2 limes
- 1 tbsp olive oil
- Salt and pepper to taste

Preparation:

1. In a large bowl, combine black beans, mangoes, bell pepper, red onion, and cilantro.
2. In a small bowl, whisk together lime juice, olive oil, salt, and pepper.
3. Pour the dressing over the salad and toss to combine.

Nutritional Information (per serving):

Calories: ~180

Protein: 5g

Carbohydrates: 33g

Fat: 3.5g

Watermelon Arugula Salad

Serving: 4

Ingredients:

- 4 cups arugula
- 2 cups watermelon, cubed
- 1/2 cup vegan feta cheese, crumbled
- 1/4 cup red onion, thinly sliced
- 1/4 cup balsamic vinegar
- 2 tbsp olive oil
- 1 tbsp maple syrup
- Salt and pepper to taste

Preparation:

1. In a large bowl, combine arugula, watermelon, vegan feta, and red onion.
2. In a small bowl, whisk together balsamic vinegar, olive oil, maple syrup, salt, and pepper.
3. Drizzle the dressing over the salad and toss gently.

Nutritional Information (per serving):

Calories: ~150

Protein: 3g

Carbohydrates: 18g

Fat: 8g

Cucumber Avocado Salad

Serving: 6

Ingredients:

- 2 cucumbers, diced
- 2 avocados, diced
- 1 cup cherry tomatoes, halved
- 1/4 cup red onion, finely chopped
- 2 tbsp fresh dill, chopped
- Juice of 1 lemon
- 2 tbsp olive oil
- Salt and pepper to taste

Preparation:

1. In a large bowl, combine cucumbers, avocados, cherry tomatoes, red onion, and dill.
2. Drizzle lemon juice and olive oil over the salad, then season with salt and pepper.
3. Gently toss to combine.

Nutritional Information (per serving):

Calories: ~180

Protein: 3g

Carbohydrates: 11g

Fat: 15g

Thai Noodle Salad

Serving: 4

Ingredients:

- 8 oz rice noodles, cooked and cooled
- 1 cup shredded carrots
- 1 cup purple cabbage, thinly sliced
- 1 red bell pepper, julienned
- 1/4 cup fresh cilantro, chopped
- 1/4 cup peanuts, chopped
- 1/4 cup lime juice
- 2 tbsp soy sauce
- 1 tbsp maple syrup
- 1 tsp sesame oil
- 1 tsp Sriracha sauce (adjust to taste)

Preparation:

1. In a large bowl, combine rice noodles, shredded carrots, purple cabbage, red bell pepper, cilantro, and peanuts.
2. In a small bowl, whisk together lime juice, soy sauce, maple syrup, sesame oil, and Sriracha.
3. Drizzle the dressing over the salad and toss to coat.

Nutritional Information (per serving):

Calories: ~300

Protein: 6g

Carbohydrates: 53g

Fat: 7g

Mediterranean Chickpea Salad

Serving: 6

Ingredients:

- 2 cans (15 oz each) chickpeas, drained and rinsed
- 1 cup cucumber, diced
- 1 cup cherry tomatoes, halved
- 1/2 cup red onion, finely chopped
- 1/2 cup Kalamata olives, pitted and halved
- 1/2 cup fresh parsley, chopped
- 1/4 cup extra-virgin olive oil
- Juice of 1 lemon
- 1 tsp dried oregano
- Salt and pepper to taste

Preparation:

1. In a large bowl, combine chickpeas, cucumber, cherry tomatoes, red onion, olives, and parsley.
2. In a small bowl, whisk together olive oil, lemon juice, dried oregano, salt, and pepper.
3. Drizzle the dressing over the salad and toss gently.

Nutritional Information (per serving):

Calories: ~300

Protein: 9g

Carbohydrates: 33g

Fat: 15g

Roasted Beet and Orange Salad

Serving: 4

Ingredients:

- 3 large beets, roasted, peeled, and cubed
- 2 large oranges, peeled and segmented
- 1/2 cup baby spinach
- 1/4 cup chopped walnuts
- 1/4 cup red onion, thinly sliced
- 2 tbsp balsamic vinegar
- 2 tbsp olive oil
- 1 tbsp maple syrup
- Salt and pepper to taste

Preparation:

1. In a large bowl, combine roasted beets, orange segments, baby spinach, walnuts, and red onion.
2. In a small bowl, whisk together balsamic vinegar, olive oil, maple syrup, salt, and pepper.
3. Drizzle the dressing over the salad and toss gently.

Nutritional Information (per serving):

Calories: ~220

Protein: 4g

Carbohydrates: 25g

Fat: 14g

Southwestern Corn Salad

Serving: 6

Ingredients:

- 4 cups cooked corn kernels (fresh or frozen)
- 1 cup black beans, drained and rinsed
- 1 red bell pepper, diced
- 1/2 cup red onion, finely chopped
- 1/4 cup fresh cilantro, chopped
- Juice of 2 limes
- 2 tbsp olive oil
- 1 tsp ground cumin
- Salt and pepper to taste

Preparation:

1. In a large bowl, combine corn kernels, black beans, red bell pepper, red onion, and cilantro.
2. In a small bowl, whisk together lime juice, olive oil, ground cumin, salt, and pepper.
3. Drizzle the dressing over the salad and toss to combine.

Nutritional Information (per serving):

Calories: ~180

Protein: 6g

Carbohydrates: 31g

Fat: 5g

Asian Slaw with Peanut Dressing

Serving: 6

Ingredients:

- 4 cups shredded cabbage (green and purple)
- 1 cup shredded carrots
- 1 red bell pepper, julienned
- 1/2 cup edamame, cooked and shelled
- 1/4 cup chopped peanuts
- 1/4 cup fresh cilantro, chopped
- 1/4 cup creamy peanut butter
- 2 tbsp rice vinegar
- 1 tbsp soy sauce
- 1 tbsp maple syrup
- 1 tsp sesame oil
- 1 clove garlic, minced

Preparation:

1. In a large bowl, combine shredded cabbage, shredded carrots, red bell pepper, edamame, chopped peanuts, and cilantro.
2. In a separate bowl, whisk together peanut butter, rice vinegar, soy sauce, maple syrup, sesame oil, and minced garlic to make the dressing.
3. Drizzle the peanut dressing over the slaw and toss well.

Nutritional Information (per serving):

Calories: ~220

Protein: 9g

Carbohydrates: 23g

Fat: 12g

Spinach Strawberry Salad

Serving: 4

Ingredients:

- 6 cups baby spinach
- 1 1/2 cups strawberries, sliced
- 1/2 cup sliced almonds
- 1/4 cup red onion, thinly sliced
- 1/4 cup balsamic vinegar
- 2 tbsp olive oil
- 1 tbsp maple syrup
- Salt and pepper to taste

Preparation:

1. In a large bowl, combine baby spinach, sliced strawberries, sliced almonds, and red onion.
2. In a small bowl, whisk together balsamic vinegar, olive oil, maple syrup, salt, and pepper.
3. Drizzle the dressing over the salad and toss gently.

Nutritional Information (per serving):

Calories: ~180

Protein: 4g

Carbohydrates: 17g

Fat: 12g

Irresistible Vegan Desserts from the Grill

Grilled Fruit Skewers with Coconut-Lime Drizzle:

Serving: 4 skewers

Ingredients:

- Assorted fruits (pineapple, mango, banana, strawberries)
- 1/4 cup coconut milk
- Zest and juice of 1 lime
- 2 tablespoons maple syrup

Preparation:

1. Preheat the grill to medium-high heat.
2. Thread the fruits onto skewers.
3. Grill the skewers for 2-3 minutes per side, until they have grill marks.
4. In a bowl, whisk together the coconut milk, lime zest, lime juice, and maple syrup.
5. Drizzle the coconut-lime mixture over the grilled fruit skewers.

Nutritional Information (per serving):

Calories: 120

Carbohydrates: 28g

Fiber: 3g

Sugar: 18g

Fat: 1g

Grilled Vegan S'mores:

Serving: 4 s'mores

Ingredients:

- Vegan marshmallows
- Vegan chocolate squares
- Vegan graham crackers

Preparation:

1. Skewer vegan marshmallows onto sticks.
2. Toast the marshmallows over the grill until they're golden brown and gooey.
3. Place a piece of vegan chocolate on a graham cracker.
4. Place the toasted marshmallow on top of the chocolate.
5. Top with another graham cracker and press to make a sandwich.

Nutritional Information (per serving):

Calories: 180

Carbohydrates: 35g

Fiber: 2g

Sugar: 17g

Fat: 5g

Grilled Cinnamon Sugar Pineapple:

Serving: 4 servings

Ingredients:

- 1 pineapple, peeled and sliced
- 2 tablespoons melted coconut oil
- 2 tablespoons brown sugar
- 1 teaspoon ground cinnamon

Preparation:

1. Preheat the grill to medium heat.
2. Brush pineapple slices with melted coconut oil.
3. In a bowl, mix brown sugar and cinnamon.
4. Grill pineapple slices for about 2-3 minutes per side, until grill marks appear.
5. Sprinkle the cinnamon sugar mixture over the grilled pineapple.

Nutritional Information (per serving):

Calories: 130

Carbohydrates: 32g

Fiber: 3g

Sugar: 24g

Fat: 2g

Grilled Banana Split:

Serving: 2 servings

Ingredients:

- 2 ripe bananas, halved lengthwise
- 1 tablespoon coconut oil
- Vegan ice cream
- Vegan chocolate sauce
- Chopped nuts and cherries for topping

Preparation:

1. Preheat the grill to medium-high heat.
2. Brush the cut side of bananas with coconut oil.
3. Grill bananas for about 2 minutes per side.
4. Serve each banana half with a scoop of vegan ice cream.
5. Drizzle with vegan chocolate sauce and top with chopped nuts and cherries.

Nutritional Information (per serving):

Calories: 280

Carbohydrates: 45g

Fiber: 5g

Sugar: 24g

Fat: 10g

Grilled Watermelon with Balsamic Glaze:

Serving: 4 servings

Ingredients:

- 1 small watermelon, sliced into rounds
- 2 tablespoons balsamic vinegar
- 1 tablespoon maple syrup
- Fresh mint leaves for garnish

Preparation:

1. Preheat the grill to medium heat.
2. Grill watermelon slices for about 2-3 minutes per side.
3. In a small saucepan, heat balsamic vinegar and maple syrup until slightly reduced.
4. Drizzle the balsamic glaze over the grilled watermelon.
5. Garnish with fresh mint leaves.

Nutritional Information (per serving):

Calories: 60

Carbohydrates: 15g

Fiber: 1g

Sugar: 12g

Fat: 0g

Grilled Peach Parfait:

Serving: 2 parfaits

Ingredients:

- 2 ripe peaches, halved and pitted
- 1 cup vegan yogurt
- 1/4 cup granola
- 2 tablespoons agave syrup

Preparation:

1. Preheat the grill to medium-high heat.
2. Grill peach halves for 2-3 minutes per side.
3. In serving glasses, layer grilled peaches, vegan yogurt, and granola.
4. Drizzle with agave syrup.

Nutritional Information (per serving):

Calories: 220

Carbohydrates: 40g

Fiber: 3g

Sugar: 26g

Fat: 4g

Grilled Coconut Pineapple Rice Pudding:

Serving: 4 servings

Ingredients:

- 1 cup cooked jasmine rice
- 1 can coconut milk
- 1/4 cup brown sugar
- 1 teaspoon vanilla extract
- 1/2 teaspoon ground cinnamon
- 1/2 cup grilled pineapple chunks

Preparation:

1. In a saucepan, combine coconut milk, brown sugar, vanilla, and cinnamon. Heat until sugar is dissolved.
2. Add cooked rice and grilled pineapple to the saucepan. Cook, stirring, until the mixture thickens.
3. Serve warm or chilled.

Nutritional Information (per serving):

Calories: 350

Carbohydrates: 45g

Fiber: 2g

Sugar: 23g

Fat: 18g

Grilled Fig and Vegan Cheese Crostini:

Serving: 6 crostini

Ingredients:

- 6 slices of baguette or ciabatta
- Vegan cream cheese or vegan ricotta
- Fresh figs, halved
- Drizzle of agave syrup
- Fresh thyme leaves for garnish

Preparation:

1. Preheat the grill to medium heat.
2. Grill bread slices until toasted on both sides.
3. Spread a layer of vegan cream cheese or ricotta on each slice.
4. Top with grilled fig halves.
5. Drizzle with agave syrup and garnish with fresh thyme leaves.

Nutritional Information (per serving):

Calories: 150

Carbohydrates: 27g

Fiber: 2g

Sugar: 10g

Fat: 3g

Grilled Apple Crisp Packets:

Serving: 4 servings

Ingredients:

- 4 apples, peeled, cored, and sliced
- 1 tablespoon lemon juice
- 1/4 cup rolled oats
- 2 tablespoons flour
- 2 tablespoons brown sugar
- 1/2 teaspoon ground cinnamon
- Pinch of salt
- 2 tablespoons vegan butter, cut into small pieces

Preparation:

1. Preheat the grill to medium-high heat.
2. Toss apple slices with lemon juice.
3. In a bowl, combine oats, flour, brown sugar, cinnamon, and salt.
4. Divide the apples between four pieces of aluminum foil.
5. Top each with the oat mixture and vegan butter.
6. Fold the foil to create packets and grill for about 15-20 minutes, until apples are tender.

Nutritional Information (per serving):

Calories: 220

Carbohydrates: 44g

Fiber: 6g

Sugar: 29g

Fat: 4g

Grilled Chocolate-Stuffed Bananas:

Serving: 4 servings

Ingredients:

- 4 ripe bananas, unpeeled
- Vegan chocolate chips
- Vegan marshmallows

Preparation:

1. Preheat the grill to medium-high heat.
2. Slice each banana lengthwise through the peel, leaving the bottom peel intact.
3. Fill the banana with vegan chocolate chips and marshmallows.
4. Wrap each banana in aluminum foil.
5. Grill for about 5-7 minutes until the chocolate and marshmallows are melted.
6. Carefully open the foil and enjoy with a spoon.

Nutritional Information (per serving):

Calories: 200

Carbohydrates: 50g

Fiber: 4g

Sugar: 30g

Fat: 1g

Printed in Great Britain
by Amazon